into History

by **Donna Watson** and
Kristin Marciniak

 HOUGHTON MIFFLIN HARCOURT
School Publishers

ILLUSTRATION CREDIT: Susan Carlson, Len Ebert

PHOTOGRAPHY CREDITS: Cover, tp © Bettmann/Corbis; 3 © Library of Congress; 5 © Retrofile/Getty Images; 6 © Bettmann/Corbis; 7 © GeoStock/Getty Images; 8, 12–14 © Bettmann/Corbis.

Printed in China

ISBN-10: 0-547-25347-8
ISBN-13: 978-0-547-25347-3

5 6 7 8 0940 18 17 16 15 14 13 12 11 10

Orville and Wilbur Wright's father had a special surprise when he came home from work one day. He brought his sons a toy made out of paper and a rubber band. When thrown into the air, it floated high in the air. Orville and Wilbur loved the toy helicopter and spent hours playing with it.

Wilbur (right) and Orville remembered their flying toy years later on, when they built their first airplane.

A Curious Pair

Wilbur was born in 1867 and Orville was born in 1871. Although they were four years apart in age, the brothers were <mark>inseparable</mark>. They loved to spend time together.

Wilbur was very hardworking. He was outgoing and enjoyed sports. Orville was the troublemaker and misbehaved in school.

Their parents enjoyed the boys' curiosity. Their mother had attended college, which was unusual for a woman at that time, and their father was a minister. He also wrote a religious newspaper.

Kite flying inspired the brothers' first airplane design.

Both of the brothers loved to try new things. Wilbur once built a machine that folded his father's newspapers so they could easily be sent to readers around the country. Orville was very interested in kites. He enjoyed making them and selling them to his friends.

New Ways to Move

In 1892, the brothers became interested in bicycles. They soon started repairing bicycles for others and opened their own bicycle shop in Dayton, Ohio, called the Wright Cycle Company. They made their own bicycles and sold them to the public. Even though the brothers enjoyed working on their bicycles, their chief interest was flying.

Bicycle riding was very popular in the 1800s.

Learning to Fly

In 1896, Orville became very ill with a high fever. During this time, Wilbur studied books and magazines about flying machines.

The brothers agreed that if birds could fly, there had to be a way for humans to fly, too. They studied bird wings and watched how birds moved them to fly.

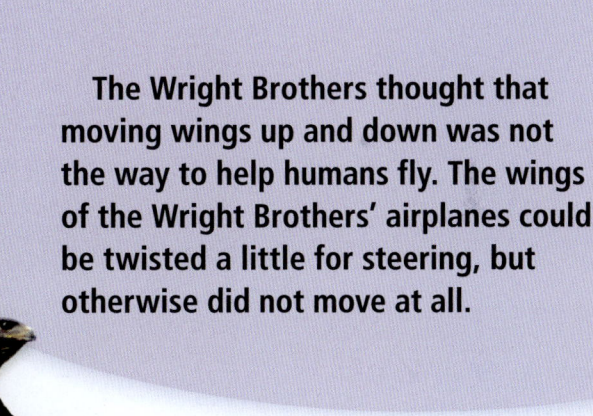

The Wright Brothers thought that moving wings up and down was not the way to help humans fly. The wings of the Wright Brothers' airplanes could be twisted a little for steering, but otherwise did not move at all.

Birds flap their wings up and down to lift their bodies into the air.

The Biplane Glider

In 1899, the Wright brothers made their first model airplane, called a biplane glider. It was made out of fabric and wood. It had two wings that were five feet long, one on top of the other. The glider worked like a giant kite.

Orville and Wilbur controlled their first airplane by pulling on strings connected to the wings.

Kitty Hawk was a good place to test their plane because it had few buildings or trees for the glider to crash into.

It took the brothers a year to make a full-sized glider. It looked very much like the model biplane glider, but its wings were 17 feet long from tip to tip. The pilot, who controls the airplane, had to lie down flat on the wings.

Many other people were trying to be the first to fly. The brothers were worried that an intruder would break in and steal their airplane design. They built an enclosure with a workshop so they could work on their airplane in private.

The brothers were having trouble making the glider stay in the air for long periods of time. It would come down with a crash. After three days, the glider finally fell apart.

Kitty Hawk, North Carolina, is 675 miles from the Wright brothers' home in Ohio. The brothers had to break their gliders into pieces and carry them on trains and boats to get to their testing area.

Another Try

Wilbur and Orville didn't give up on their dream to fly. In 1902, they made a glider that had longer wings and a moveable tail to help with steering. It worked better than the first glider, but the brothers knew it would need an engine and propellers to stay in the air.

The Wright Brothers' 1903 airplane had a small, lightweight engine and two large propellers.

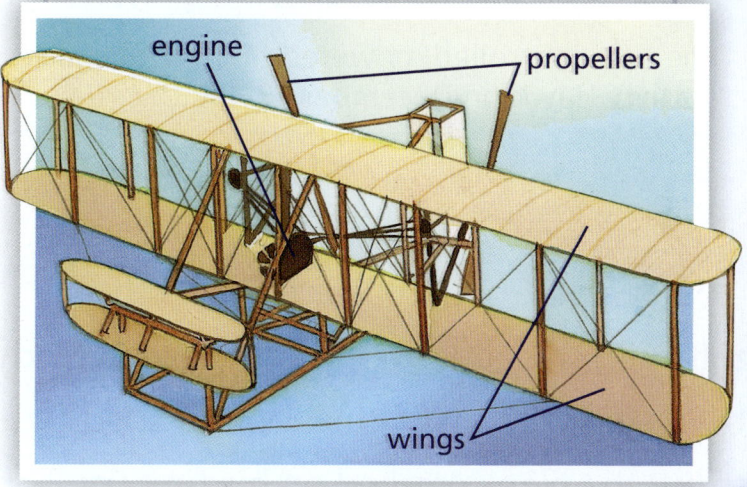

engine

propellers

wings

A mechanic named Charlie Taylor helped the Wright Brothers build the engine, which had much less power than the engine in a car today.

The first controlled, powered flight took place at Kitty Hawk on December 17, 1903.

Exhausted from thousands of practice flights with the glider, the brothers were ready to try flying with an engine. Wilbur tried flying first, but the plane crashed on his first try. Three days later, on December 17, 1903, Orville made history by lifting an airplane with an engine off the ground for the first time.

The Wright brothers continued to work on their airplanes. They would be amazed if they knew how important their invention has become for travel all over the world today.

Wilbur and Orville were very smart and determined. However, their father often said that neither of them could have done it without the other. They were true friends.

The Wright brothers made a great team.

The Wright Brothers' Path to Flight

1867 — Wilbur Wright was born.

1871 — Orville Wright was born.

1878 — Their father gave them a toy helicopter made out of paper and a rubber band.

1892 — The brothers opened Wright Cycle Company in Dayton, Ohio.

1899 — Orville and Wilbur built a small biplane kite.

1900 — The brothers spent a year making their first full-size biplane glider. Its wings were 17 feet across.

1903 — The brothers decide to put a small engine in an airplane they called "The Flyer."

Dec. 17, 1903 — Orville made the first successful powered flight. It was 12 seconds long and the plane flew 120 feet.

Responding

TARGET SKILL **Compare and Contrast**

How successful were the Wright brothers at flying before they tried engine power? What changed after they tried engine power? Copy and complete the chart below.

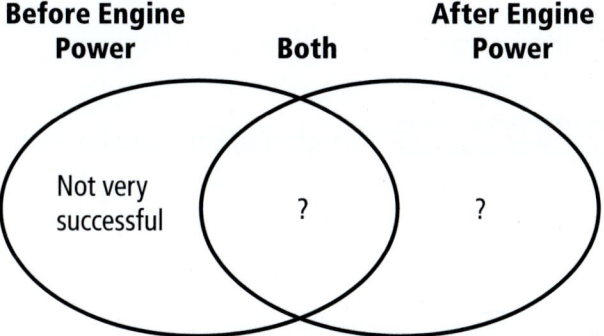

Before Engine Power	Both	After Engine Power
Not very successful	?	?

 Write About It

Text to World Write an informative paragraph describing how the invention of the airplane has made it easier to travel. Use words such as *first*, *next*, and *finally* to help order your ideas.

affection
bond
charged
chief
companion

enclosure
exhausted
inseparable
intruder
suffered

TARGET SKILL **Compare and Contrast** Examine how details or ideas are alike or different.

TARGET STRATEGY **Analyze/Evaluate** Think carefully about the text and form an opinion about it.

GENRE Narrative Nonfiction gives factual information by telling a true story.